amanda
May the angels
above bless
you.
Fr. Craig
†

Angel Girl

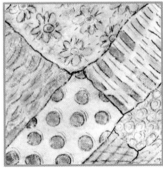

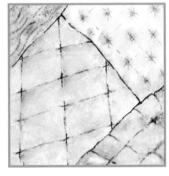

Written by Fr. Craig Harrison
Illustrated by Linda Brown

DORRANCE PUBLISHING CO., INC.
PITTSBURGH, PENNSYLVANIA 15222

For more information or to order additional books, please contact:
Dorrance Publishing Co., Inc.
701 Smithfield Street
Third Floor
Pittsburgh, Pennsylvania 15222
U.S.A.
1-800-788-7654
www.dorrancebookstore.com

Dedicated to all God's Angels

Aravid "Andy" Allen, Lynette Allen, Laurano Martiza Andradre, Antuna, Peter Antuna, Barajas, Juan Barajaz, Virginia Beal, Matthew Celeste Bernal, Mark Jeffrey Border, Gabrielle Brown, Neal Bursey, Brandon Timothy Carr, Danny Castillo, Cervantes, Krysta Rose Chaidez, Margaret Cortez, Evan Cousineau, Eddie Dean, Tom Debeau, Dominic

Santana Peter Antongiovanni, Alejandro Arana, Brian Christian Barrett, Robert Beal, Jr., Craig Beers, Sophia Blanchard, Jr., Marko Bonilla, Eva Ann Bowyer, Kevin Boylan, Lori Cagle, Melissa Calderon, Susan Athena Cervantes, Christophe Amy Chamberlain, Leticia Tim Cutler, Michelle Joseph DeBondt,

Jean Andrade, Marcos G. Banducci, Alfredo "Bobby" Battistone, Bella, Brock Bellue, Borba, Chloe Border, Brock, Samuel Anthony Cardella, Jesus Cardenas, Cervantes, Noemi Alaniz Chavez, Deardre Clark, Davenport, Angelina Dazzo, Mary Elizabeth DeBondt, Joseph

Benjaman DeCordova III, Steven DeMarco, Thomas Demler, Jegs Lapena Diego, Barnardino Dionisla, Lynn Dira, Marilyn Victoria Dixon, Anthony Dumas, Branna Lynn Dunn, Jacob Duran, Tim Durando, Rickey Elrod, Erick Escobar, Katrina Estrada, John Michael Fachin, William Bret Fields, Shana Finch, Brook Finn, Jackie Tozzi Franconi, Caleb Gamboa, Destiny Garcia, George Garcia, Teri Garcia, Joseph Getty, Clark Gimena, Christopher Gomez, Patricia Gomez, Athena A. Gonzales, Jose Gonzales, Ramon Gonzales, Mia Gonzalez, Dennis Goodell, Jeff Graves, Benjamin Grider, Lillian Grace Grider, Juan G. Guerrero, Jeffrey Donald Harrison, Nancy Harrison-Frey, Joseph William Harvey, Juan Jose Hernandez, Matthew Cole Hernandez, Sydney Hernandez, Arrianna Heredia, George Herrera, Tiffany Herrera, Dana Kristine Hilderbrandt, John Hillman, Brittany Marie Holland, Miguel Angel Izaguire, Neracla Kano, James Johnson, Kathleen Johnson, Kim Juarez, Wayne Keenan, Jonathan Kennon, Jeannie Kirkpatrick, Jeny Klawitter, Nicholas Augustine Klein, Sara Magdalene Klein, Jennifer June Knight, Brian Korger, Hollis LaBorde, Thomas Ladeusier, Taylor Elizabeth Lamb, Andrew Le, Diego Licon Leal, Andrew Lee, Fernando Levario, Jesslyn Lomas, Christopher Lopez, Mia Lopez, John Joseph "JJ" Lopez, Nevaeh Macias, Samantha Mancha, Tess Marane, Lee Roy Marshall, Roy Lee Marshall, Izabella Marquez, Jessica Martinez, Olivia Martinez, Marissa Marie Mata, Jose Pedro Mendroza, Jayleen Meza, Lucca Matteo Minnite, Dino Molina, Matthew Monreal, Mariah Andie Monzon, Michell Marina Monzon, John Bryan Moralez, Kamon Moralez, Noah Munoz, Sofia Munoz, Carlos Negrete, Alexander John Ochoa, Jordan Ochoa, Larry Olcott, Matthew O'Reilly, Daniel Ornelas, Ralph Pacini, Lea Pascual, Christine Ann Perez, Rolando Perez, Michelle Peters, Kellie Lynn Petris, Rocco Poppa, Rebekka Lynn Potter, David Powell, Enrique Prieto, Mazzie Prince, Sarah Wiswall Pudiwiter, Augustine Ramirez, Jose Miguel Ramirez, John M. Ramirez, Jr., Lance Lane Ratcliff, Stacey Ray, Gracianna Register, David Reischman, Issac Rhinehart, Dean Right, Samantha Rios, Desiree Rivera, Gabriella Rodriguez, Daniela Rosales, Diana Rosales, Andrea Monique Ruiz, Andrew Martin Ruiz, Guillermo Ruiz, Raul Ruiz, Nabor Lopez Salcedo, Frank Sanchez, Jr., Jane Jenner Schlemper, Darah Schulte, Alyssa Segoviano, Audrey Lynn Serban, Benjamin Aaron Serban, Jean Catherine Serban, Lisa Christine Serban, Michael Shelton, Mayson Shuck, George Caratan Sill, William Sing, Lauren Small, Maggie Small, Mark Small, Kory Ray Snook, Daniel Solis, Lantz Spears, Brandon Spurgin, Jeff Stanley, Shawn Patrick Sullivan, Robert Swoboda, Gerardo Tapia, Jr., Joshua Taylor, Victoria Diane Taylor, Susan Tazioli, Marie Thomas, Meghan Thomas, Rosie Perez Thomas, Sean Thomas, Sarah Tobias, Tim Torigiani, Alexis Torres, Lizette Torres, Ryan Alexander Torres, Marisela Trujillo, Sesilia Valencia, Michael James Valenti, Chelsi Valverde, Gregory VanDerVoon, Daniel Luke Vara, Matthew James Vargra, Jack Vasquez, Stephen Vasquez, Fred Velasquez, Juan Velasquez, Chelsea Velverde, Jose B. Verduzco, Maria Verduzco, Francisco Villa, Ruby Vlega, Corey Wahl, Brandon Wedel, Brian Weldin, Jennifer Marie White, Addison Elaine Widhalm, Dean Wright, Steven Zambrano

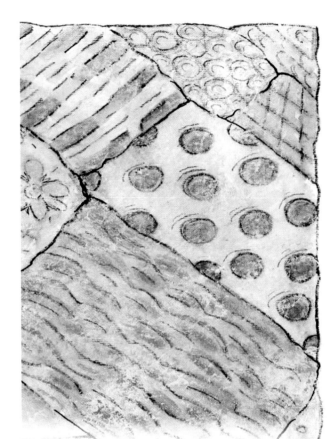

I want to tell you a true story that never happened........or did it?

Once upon a time, a trillion years ago in forever, God called a meeting of all the unborn children. There were millions of kids.

God said, "I am going to have a contest. It is a very special contest because the winner of the contest will receive the title of ANGEL GIRL."

The boys were really MAD!

God continued, "The rules are simple. This contest is about love. You must teach it to everyone – family, friends and even the world. I won't give extra help; but I will always be with you. Know if you choose to enter this contest it may not be easy. You could face hard times and disappointments but never give up if you want the title of ANGEL GIRL."

I thought, "This is for me!"

Then God added, "You might find clues on the way. Oh, yes, there is one more rule – IT MUST BE A SECRET. You cannot let anyone know you are trying to win heaven's greatest award!"

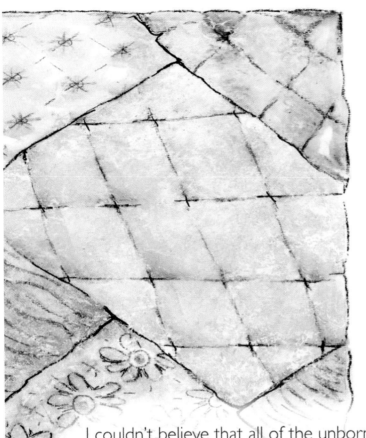

I couldn't believe that all of the unborn children didn't jump at the chance to play the game! Me, I couldn't wait! I wanted to win the contest. I wasn't sure how I was going to win – I just knew I was going to be the next ANGEL GIRL.

All the unborn got very quiet then God said, "On your mark, get ready, get set and go!"

I was sent to the Small family. I was given a brother, a mom, a dad, a crazy aunt and some old people called "grandparents". I was all red and wrinkly but they loved me immediately. I came home from the hospital in my father's arms. My mother fed me and changed me and gave me tickle scratches all the time. My brother would just stare at me and make faces.

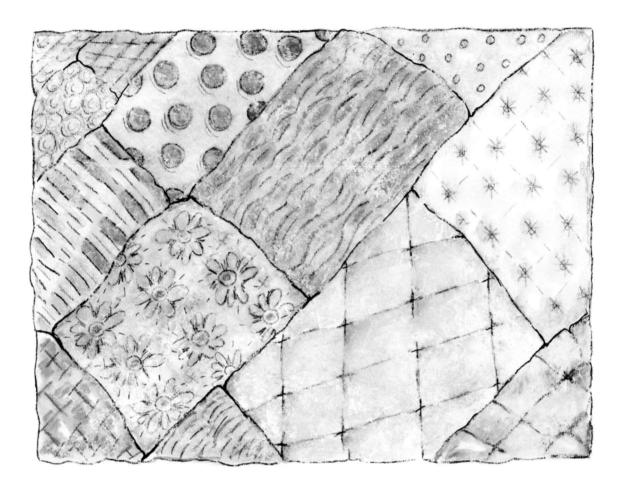

My family was very easy to love. This contest seemed so easy I thought I would win hands down! Even my brother knew I was special; he never beat me up or hid my dolls.

As I grew older, still secretly working on being ANGEL GIRL, I knew I had to teach love to my classmates, friends and neighbors. I tried different ideas and even learned about love from my friends. I was blessed with a loving world.

Something told me I had to do more to earn the title. I had to find others to love and share this gift. I needed to have a plan. I needed a challenge.

I wanted to tell Mom and Dad about the contest but that was a rule, "no spilling the beans!" I needed something to show the world how strong I was and willing to bring love to the world. I waited for God's clue.

Our family loved horses and my dad, a pushover for his children, bought me a horse. I practiced and rode tall winning many contests and awards. I was good. I mean really good. I met many great people. I used my gifts well – swimming, tennis and loving food (eating that is, not cooking!)

I even went to dance class with boys, but there was no love there.

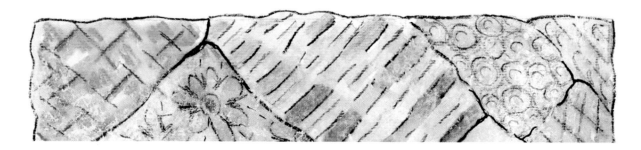

I was getting really worried because it was too easy for me to love and be loved. To win the contest I had to reach the lonely, sad and even the angry people and teach them to love.

I had to make a plan. A really good plan.

One day as I was going over my ideas for the plan I got sick. It wasn't a little sickness: I was not getting better. I asked, "Why am I sick, God? I have been trying so hard. Why did you make me sick?"

God answered, "I did not make you sick. I made you perfect." Then He smiled at me and added, "Maybe being sick will help you learn more about love."

I thought, "Is this a clue for the ANGEL GIRL contest?"

I did not understand how my sickness was going to help me win the contest but I wasn't going to let this illness stop me from winning the game.

My Mom and Dad took me all over the world to various doctors. They tried everything to make me better. What they did not know was they were giving me power. I felt determined to continue spreading love.

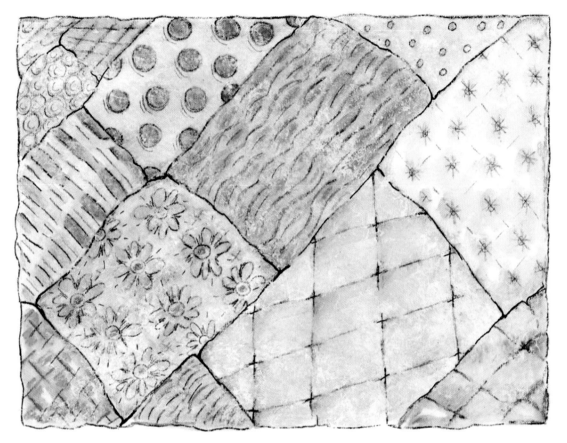

Don't get me wrong; some of the people I met on my trips weren't easy. People in hospitals are sad and frightened. I was frightened too but maybe there are clues in being scared.

The medical staff poked me and probed me. It was a challenge to think of love when I had to swallow the awful medicine.

Through it all I kept thinking about being crowned ANGEL GIRL in heaven.

God would visit me all the time – I never felt alone. God asked me, "Do you want to quit the game? I know you are very sick and very tired."

But I told God as long as He was near I would never give up.

My Mom and Dad brought my pastor, a kind and gentle man, to see me. He Baptized me and I knew I saw God smile. I was so happy and I knew He was too.

Sometimes I would get sad thinking about how my body was getting in the way of my plan. I couldn't ride horses anymore or go to school with my friends. My Mom would not let me be sad. She would say, "C'mon. Let's take another trip. We have some new people for you to meet."

I told God I would never give up. My Mom and Dad were helping me so much. I really wanted to tell them about the ANGEL GIRL contest so they could help me with a plan.

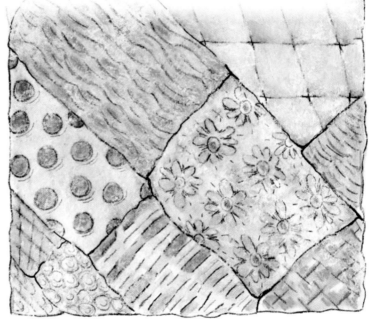

Then everything started to make sense. *I knew how I was going to win the contest!*

It wouldn't be easy but I knew I could pull it off. I got a wonderful clue from my family. I wanted so badly to tell my brother. He will just have to wait for the ANGEL BOY contest.

Everyone was concerned about my sickness. Many, many friends and family came to comfort my Mom and Dad.

I felt for them and loved them but now I had a plan. The plan would make me win so I could have a special title in heaven.

I remember my last day so well!

My room was filled with love. My parents, grandparents, neighbors and friends were in my room. My brother came home from school to be with me (I really think he liked getting out of school).

There was a tap on the door and my Dad brought my pastor up to my bed. In his hands he held the special gift of my First Holy Communion. When I received Jesus I knew my plan was complete.

"Soon I will be crowned ANGEL GIRL". I said in a voice that no one heard.

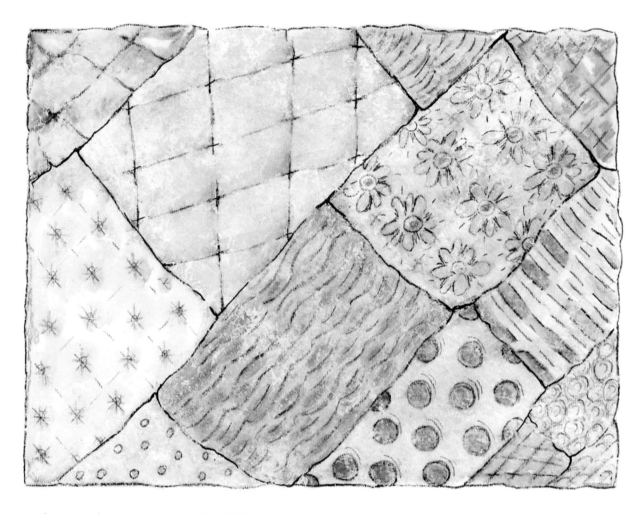

It was time to share MY SPECIAL PLAN. It was unique. It was really me!

I looked around. My stuffed animals seemed to be looking at me. I bet they knew. After all God loves all His creations—even those with button eyes I thought!

The first thing I had to do was to get rid of this body because it was slowing me down. My parents were holding me but before I drew my last breath I squeezed their wrist three times and they squeezed me back three times.

We had done this throughout my life. It means I LOVE YOU!

Everyone in heaven was watching me. They saw my family so sad and watched my Dad carrying my body out of the house. He loved me so much from the time he first carried me into the house years ago. I was so proud of my parents. Mom held my hand and never made me feel alone.

Everyone thought it was over but that was the brilliance of my plan!

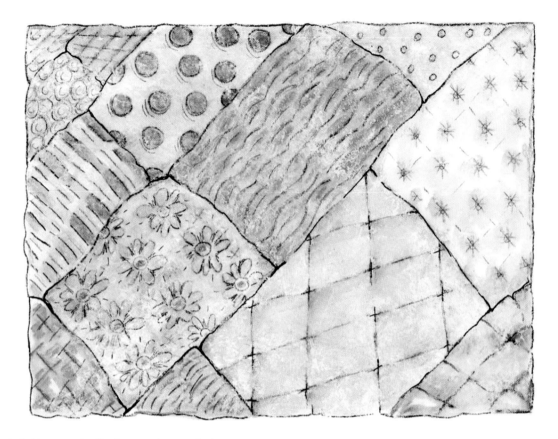

I followed all the rules of the contest.

First of all I brought people together. How did I do that?

I got them to come to church for my services! (I fooled some of them, as they hadn't been in a church for years). I know God was happy about that!

But there was more to my plan! And you are part of it!

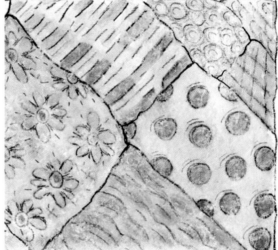

Now, please follow these directions carefully because I just have to win.

It is important you do this:

> Take the wrist of a person near you.
> Hold it firmly.
> Now squeeze it three times slowly.
> The three squeezes mean I LOVE YOU.

I used this with my brother, mom and dad before we went to bed every night.

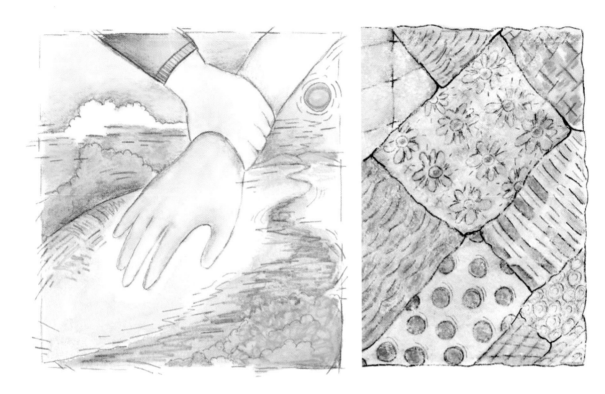

Please do this again for me. Moms and Dads do this to your children every day. You can never tell your kids you love them enough.

Squeeze the wrists of your friends, classmates and the people you meet.

Everyone needs love.

THIS IS THE ONLY THING GOD WANTS US TO DO, SPREAD HIS LOVE.

THAT IS WHY WE WERE CREATED.

Did you hear the bells? Listen! The angels are ringing the bells!

I WON! I did it – I am the new ANGEL GIRL in heaven.

Thanks to all of you I won. Mom and Dad deserve special thanks – thanks also to my many wonderful friends. You all helped me too. I am the happiest girl in heaven.

Life is exciting and God is always with you. But remember we are all created to teach love and that is the most important thing we do.

Remember, when you squeeze a wrist you are changing the world. You're telling someone you love them and that they are very important.

Pass my plan on. You will make people smile and hearts will heal.

I have to go now. Being ANGEL GIRL is very demanding. Pray for me. I will wait for you in heaven.

This is the end of my story – fooled you again!

It is just the beginning of my life in heaven. God is here with me. I am not lonely or sad.

Heaven is the perfect home for ANGEL GIRL!

Artwork above produced by Mary Pierini Allen, the mother of two of God's Angels.

Lauren Paige Small

Lauren Small was born August 1st, 1994 in Bakersfield, California. She lived with her parents Kevin and Tuesdy and a brother Kyle. She had a dog named Primer, three cats, (Allie, Cali, and Sam), two horses, (Nickie her show horse and Fancie her two year old. Lauren loved animals and wanted to become a veterinarian.

In April of 2003 Lauren broke her leg snow skiing and six weeks later was diagnosed with Osteosarcoma (bone cancer). For two years Lauren battled with the cancer, while still trying to live her life to the fullest. In January of 2005 Lauren was re-diagnosed with cancer, this time in her lungs. Lauren died December 1st, 2005.

Lauren lived each day of her life to the fullest. She was kind and loving to everyone. Her smile and vibrant personality were contagious. We are so blessed to have had her in our lives. The message of her life lives on each and every day.

The Small Family

Thank you to:

The Kevin Small Family
Judy Jacobs
My parents, family &
parish